Sandaoling

Hami

Shiguai

Baotou

Beijing

Tianjin

Dawukou

Xihe

Handan

Rujigou

Baiyin

Xingyang

Yaojie

Xuchang

Hekounan

Pingdingshan

Lanzhou

Xi'an

Shanghai

Wuhan

Chengdu

Shibanxi

Chongqing

Huangjinggou

Ganshui

Chenzhou

Pingshi

Hechi

Hong Kong

Nanning

CHINA - South, Central, West

● Featured locations

CHINA
THE WORLD´S LAST STEAM RAILWAY

A PHOTOGRAPHIC ESSAY BY
JOHN TICKNER GORDON EDGAR ADRIAN FREEMAN

CHINA

THE WORLD´S LAST STEAM RAILWAY

A PHOTOGRAPHIC ESSAY BY
JOHN TICKNER GORDON EDGAR ADRIAN FREEMAN

CHINA

THE WORLD'S LAST STEAM RAILWAY

John Tickner Gordon Edgar Adrian Freeman

Published by
AAPPL Artists' and Photographers' Press Ltd.
Church Farm House, Wisley, Surrey GU23 6QL, UK
info@aappl.com   www.aappl.com

Sales and Distribution
UK and Export: Turnaround Publisher Services Ltd.
orders@turnaround-uk.com

USA & Canada: Sterling Publishing Inc.
sales@sterlingpub.com

Australia & New Zealand: Peribo Pty Ltd.
michael.coffey@peribo.com.au

South Africa: Trinity Books
trinity@iafrica.com

A catalogue record for this book is available from the British Library.

ISBN 9781904332800

Design (contents and cover): Stefan Nekuda
office@nekuda.at

Printed in Malaysia by: Imago Publishing
info@imago.co.uk

Half title page: Passenger train near Yamenmiao. JiTong, January 2005. JT
Title page: Sunrise at Xigou. JiTong, November 2005. GE

Contents

Iced drivers - QJ 6887 at Da'an Bei, March 2000. AF

Introduction

Gordon, John and Adrian met and came to know each other on visits to China to photograph steam. Interested in railways since childhood, their horizons gradually spread beyond what was on offer in Britain.

Main line steam in Britain finished in 1968, the year that Gordon left school. He then travelled up and down the country photographing industrial steam railways. His taste for foreign steam was acquired whilst in the army in Germany during the early 1970s (West German main line steam ended in 1976, East Germany – so close but frustratingly out-of-bounds for him whilst in the army – survived until 1988) but family commitments pushed it down his list of priorities for the next 20 years.

John had also witnessed British main line steam as a schoolboy and has a handful of black and white prints, taken with his totally inadequate Kodak Brownie camera to show for it. He then developed an interest in rock climbing and railways took a back seat until the mid 1980s. He made the first of several long haul trips to India for steam in 1989.

Adrian was oblivious to the end of British main line steam, just having finished his first year at primary school. After an apprenticeship with industrial locomotive builders Hunslet Engine Company in Leeds, he spent four years at university. During his holidays, he travelled around much of Europe using 'Interrail' passes. An article in a national newspaper in 1994 stating that Indian Railways intended to get rid of all of their steam locomotives by the end of that year brought it home to him that time was running out for steam the world over. Fortunately for him, Indian Railways didn't meet their target date, but when he got there in 1995, not much was left.

China was regarded as a country that could be visited after going everywhere else for steam – that it would be the last country to get rid of steam locomotives. This view has turned out to be correct – by the start of the 21st century, steam had been largely displaced from its last strongholds in South Africa, Zimbabwe, India, Myanmar and its seasonal use in the Cuban sugar industry. The scale of steam working in China is only a tiny fraction of that of a decade ago, but with no real competition, there remains more in China than anywhere else in the world.

Adrian and Gordon made their first visit to China in March 1997 when, on an organised trip, they were paired up to share hotel rooms. With their mutual preference for skipping breakfast with the group and getting to the lineside for photography by the first light of the day, they formed a friendship which saw them make a series of return trips to China over the following years. John first visited China in February 1998, when he boldly travelled alone for a fortnight around the North-East before joining a small group for a further two weeks. He met Adrian on a later trip in 1998 and again a common interest in getting the most out of the early

QJ 6247 crosses Singing Sands viaduct on the Baotou to Shenmu local railway with coal empties, December 2000. AF

morning and late afternoon light emerged.

During our trips to China, the authors have witnessed much more than the disappearance of the steam locomotive. The country is in the throes of great change. Modernisation coupled with unprecedented economic growth is transforming the country at a terrific rate. Uncomplicated by sentimentality, complex planning permission or land ownership issues, swathes of the old China are being swept away. The country is intent on modernising, whatever the cost. A good transport infrastructure is essential for economic growth and China's railway network plays a crucial role. Although China's road network is growing rapidly, the large majority of long distance freight is carried by the railways. As the demands on the railway system increase – each year freight tonnages and passenger numbers grow – the railway has been forced to modernise, run faster trains and build new lines to cope with the demand.

China was the last country in the world to build steam locomotives. The final main line engines emerged from Datong workshops in December 1988 and production of steam locomotives for industrial use continued intermittently until September 1999.

From over 4000 steam locos in service on China Rail, the state-run national railway system at the beginning of 1996, the numbers dropped to single figures by the end of 2002. The final few were withdrawn in 2003 making China the world's last country to use steam on its main lines (India's last main line steam engines bowed out in early 2000). During this period, approximately 1000 new diesel and electric locomotives have been built each year. This has been necessary not only to

The points must be kept clear of snow and ice to keep trains running. Ice breaking, Shuangyashan yard, December 2000. GE

Large numbers of steam locomotives were bought by industrial users, primarily coal mines and steelworks. Most of these were the standard industrial engine, the SY class, but smaller numbers of the JS and QJ classes also found their way into industry, either bought new, or second hand from China Rail. Many of the industrial railway systems, particularly the colliery systems, were extensive and some ran passenger services. Shuangyashan in the far North-East was one such system. It ran 11-coach passenger trains, which until dieselisation in 2002 were hauled by QJs. All of China's surviving standard gauge steam is to be found in industry.

There was once a considerable number of narrow gauge lines in China with a concentration of forestry systems in the North-East. By the mid 1990s many of these had closed and the last steam-hauled forestry line finished in 2003 as China realised that deforestation was having a serious impact on the environment. Although almost all the narrow gauge lines used the same type of locomotive, the C2, each system had its own unique charm and character. In addition to logs, other systems shown in this book were used for coal, limestone and clay. Very few steam-hauled narrow gauge lines remain, and each of these leads a precarious existence with the ever present threat of closure. Perhaps the most charming of all of these is a line in Sichuan province at Shibanxi. Passenger and coal trains run through a hilly area yet to be penetrated by roads and motor vehicles, the passenger trains using home-made coaches. At the end of the line, tubs on still narrower gauge tracks are pushed by hand from a coal mine to the railway loading point.

Steam locomotives can still be found at a number of industrial sites scattered across the country such as mines, steelworks and factories but their numbers decline every month. It is estimated that approx. 400 steam locomotives remained in active industrial use at the beginning of 2007. However, many of these operations have recently bought or plan to buy diesels to replace their steam fleets. Even coal mines with their free fuel supply for steam locomotives are showing their determination to modernise by buying diesels. Several years ago, China declared that it would get rid of all its steam locomotives by the time it hosts the Olympics in 2008. With the possible exception of a handful of remote industrial operations, it appears to be on course to achieve this target. When this happens, it will be the end of the world's last mecca for fans of 'real' steam (commercial rather than preserved or museum operations) and scenes such as those shown in these pages will be history.

The photographs in this book were taken over the ten-year period from March 1997 to January 2007. Although the authors missed much of the main line steam working in China, there was one benefit of this late start - the freedom to go where we pleased. In the early 1980s, when China started allowing tourists in, they were not allowed to 'do their own thing', but were ushered between places that the authorities wanted foreign visitors to see. Many of the early groups of steam enthusiasts found the arrangements very frustrating with enforced lengthy stops at restaurants consuming time that could have been spent by the lineside. There were many 'closed' areas of the country where foreigners were not permitted.

replace steam but to cope with growing traffic and the opening of new lines. Since the start of the new millennium, over 5000 kilometres of new lines have been opened and many existing lines have had their capacity increased. The speeding up of passenger and freight services has been part of this capacity increase and one of the reasons for steam's demise. By 1997 steam had largely been displaced from China Rail's main lines and was generally confined to a number of secondary and branch lines, predominantly in the North-East. The final straw was the electrification of the main line between Beijing, Shenyang and Harbin, which was completed late in 2001. Electric locomotives replaced the diesels operating over this busy line and these in turn were cascaded to wipe out the few remaining pockets of steam operation.

Some of China Rail's redundant steam locomotives were sold to local railways or industry. Local railways were funded and run provincially, rather than by the state, but some were large operations such as the 300-kilometre long Sanshui Xi to Maoming Dong line in Guangdong province and the 945-kilometre long Jining Nan to Tongliao line in Inner Mongolia. This latter line was by far the best known local railway and opened as late as 1995 using ex-China Rail steam locomotives of the QJ class.

By the late 1990s things had changed considerably and individual travellers could make their own arrangements and move around much more freely. Many railway lines are used as unofficial paths by the locals and walking anywhere alongside the lines is regarded as quite normal. Indeed there is much more freedom to explore the railways and their infrastructure in this police state than there is in the security guard state that the UK has become in recent years.

In some of the more remote places foreigners would attract a lot of attention, but this was generally curiosity rather than hostility. Outposts of steam operations were often in areas way off the beaten track for most foreign visitors and on occasions, we and other railway enthusiasts were the first foreigners that some of these places had ever seen – quite extraordinary given the constant stream of backpackers now a regular sight in some of the more touristy areas. A snag was that the curiosity of local police could be attracted and trying to convey the message of what we wanted to do, when they had never seen foreigners and never heard of anyone showing interest in steam railways, could be too much for them to grasp. Having a Chinese guide would come in useful in these circumstances. Often postcards from home with pictures of steam locomotives did the trick and numerous policemen have walked away, smiling and with a couple of postcards in their hand. It was rare to find anyone that spoke English, although when John visited the city of Fuxin, the hotel manager could speak some English and expressed his amazement that he had turned up without a Chinese guide, and said he was the first Westerner to do so.

The authors travelled around China sometimes with, but mostly without, the assistance of Chinese guides. Although many places were perfectly accessible simply by turning up unannounced and making our own way around on foot, using public transport or taxi, there were occasions where guides were useful, such as gaining entry to steelworks, which had to be arranged in advance. Many other like-minded railway enthusiasts, who have travelled round China have reported what they saw and how to get there, and most of the pictures in this book couldn't have been taken without the help of this information. Although failing to get to grips with the Chinese language and the written characters, the authors built up a stock of useful travel information, including written names of dishes they particularly liked at restaurants, and forms for ordering railway tickets, so that most of the time the basics of accommodation, food and transport were not too problematic. As Don White, another of our travelling companions, pointed out "it is more important to know the system than to know the language".

The majority of our visits to China have taken us to the North-East during winter, when the temperature was extremely cold. There were a few reasons for this:
- there was a greater concentration of known systems using steam here than any other part of China,
- the colder it was, the more impressive the steam exhaust from the locomotives,
- there was a good chance of snow, which could hide much of the sometimes appalling amounts of litter and rubbish, and transform otherwise mundane scenes into appealing views,

Labourers clearing snow at Benxi steelworks, December 2004. JT

- the weather tended to be better with longer periods of high pressure and sunshine,
- low winter light is more attractive than high sunlight for photography,
- the narrow gauge logging lines only operated during the winter season.

The disadvantage of the cold was that both we and our equipment were subjected to these harsh conditions with the result that on occasions neither worked very well. Probably the coldest time was during a visit by Adrian and Gordon in the winter of 2000-1, when the temperature was regularly below -40°C on a morning.

Over the period we visited China, the exchange rate between British sterling and the Chinese Yuan has varied between 12 and 15 Yuan to the pound. In US dollars, the rate was fixed at 8.28 until July 2005 before declining to around 7.8 by the time of our last trip in January 2007.

At the date of writing there remain a number of fascinating steam operations in China but this number is steadily declining and sadly the majority of scenes in this book are already history. The authors hope that readers will enjoy these photographs, scenes of an almost extinct era, of China – the world's last steam railway.

Jalainur 'hole' – a huge opencast coal mine near the Russian border. Spoil and coal trains zig-zag back and forth between levels to get in and out, December 2005. AF

Tonghua & Hunjiang

Both Tonghua and Hunjiang are small industrial cities in Jilin province and are linked by a railway line which branches south-east off the main China Rail system at Meihekou. One of Tonghua's few claims to fame was in the production of wine, with which it had some success in the 1980s and '90s. The consumption of wine in China is very limited – it is not part of the culture – and the consumption of what most Europeans would recognise as wine is much less still. Tonghua Red was a rather sweet and sticky wine somewhat akin to a children's fruit drink but with a medicinal aftertaste. It is no longer believed to be in production. Taking the train on from Tonghua for 60 kilometres through attractive tree-covered hills, the traveller arrives at Hunjiang. The translation of the name Hunjiang approximates to 'dirty river', a name that the city's authorities decided was unsatisfactory so they renamed it Baishan, or 'white mountain'. At the time of the authors' visits, they concluded that the former name was the most appropriate, and the name Hunjiang still appears in the China Rail timetable.

China Rail's standard steam freight locomotive, the QJ class, had a long fixed wheelbase and was banned from use on this line due to the sharp curvature on the section from Tonghua to Hunjiang and beyond. Consequently the area became one of the last on China Rail to use the smaller and distinctive JS class locomotives with large smoke deflectors, built in the late 1950s and early '60s. Although the motive power in latter years was a mix of diesels and steam, the JS class managed to survive here almost to the end of main line steam on China Rail. Towards the very end, a number of much newer JS, from a batch constructed between 1986 and 1988 with smaller smoke deflectors, were transferred to this line to replace some of the older engines. In the depths of winter, it was clear that these newer engines were in a better mechanical condition as unlike many of the older engines, they hardly leaked any steam.

Songshuzhen yard and JS8208, January 2001. GE

At Tonghua, there was an engine shed built by the Japanese in the 1930s in the form of a part roundhouse with turntable, but facilities at Hunjiang were rather more basic with no undercover accommodation for the JS and a triangle to turn the locomotives. JS class without deflectors were based at Tonghua and Hunjiang to shunt the goods yards and to work coal trains along the Hunjiang power station branch. In the last years of their operation, the JS class were mostly used on freight duties but one of their last regular passenger train workings was the 15:43 from Hunjiang to Songshuzhen, on the Baihe line; two of the authors' winter visits were carefully timed to be sure its departure could be photographed just before sunset.

There was a busy level crossing on the power station branch. One night, during our stay, the crossing keeper fell asleep and failed to lower the barriers when a train was due. The train hit a lorry on the crossing and pushed it into the crossing keeper's hut, demolished it and injured the crossing keeper. We saw the hut next morning as a pile of rubble. Later that afternoon, as we headed down for the passenger departure, the rubble had been cleared and eight courses of bricks had been laid. By the time we returned, the windows were in. During the course of the next day, after a freezing night which will surely have done wonders for

JS 8040 departs Songshuzhen for Hunjiang, January 2001. AF

Steep gradients north of Songshuzhen meant that even short freights needed double-heading. JS 8208 and 8042 wait to depart, January 2001. GE

the setting mortar, we saw at various times, the walls finished, the roof go on, and finally the walls being rendered. All within 48 hours of the original accident! We were informed that once the crossing keeper had been released from hospital, she would be 'severely criticised'!

At the Baihe end of Hunjiang station was a bridge over the river; at the Tonghua end, a level crossing, both of which afforded good photographic opportunities. One morning in winter we were standing on the road looking towards this level crossing; the view was in the direction of the rising sun. Pollution could be a wonderful thing for putting colour into the sky, particularly at sunrise and sunset and this spot benefited considerably from the smog. Waiting at the edge of the road for shapes of JS locomotives to cross in front of us, we observed the daily routines of numerous Chinese: three-wheeler taxis pottering up and down the road looking for business, the lady pushing her barrow of steaming bean curd complete with megaphone and pre-recorded tape-loop message advertising her ware, shops and stalls setting up for the day's business, and children on their way

to school. The schoolchildren were learning English at school. One bolder child dared to speak to us: Where did we come from? What were our names? Then to John: "How old are you?" "Very old" came the reply (he was in his mid forties at the time). Apparently satisfied with the answers, the children disappeared. Minutes later however, one of the children returned with his mother, who was carrying a chair. It was placed next to John, who was invited to sit down. Totally embarrassed by this act of respect, the offer was sheepishly declined. Such behaviour would be unheard of back home.

Plans to visit this area again in January 2002 never came to fruition when the authors picked up the news a few days before their intended visit that it had been dieselised. Unbeknown to them at the time, a number of JS class soldiered on further up the line on the steeply graded section between Songshuzhen and Baihe until March 2002, one of the final places to employ regular steam traction on China Rail.

JS 6315 eastbound at Liudaojiang village between Tonghua and Hunjiang, November 1999. JT

An unidentified JS leaves Hunjiang with the 15:43
passenger to Songshuzhen, November 1999. JT

(right) JS 6483 on a morning departure from Hunjiang
crossing the frozen river, January 2001. AF

The level crossing at the Tonghua end of Hunjiang station, November 1999. AF

Morning smog at Hunjiang level crossing, January 2001. GE

JS 8040 pulls away from Songshuzhen with a westbound freight, January 2001. GE

JS 8234 takes the first train of the day down the Hunjiang power station branch after overnight snow, January 2001. AF

An unidentified JS crosses the river at Hunjiang on empties, January 2001. GE

JS 5678, 5855 & 5413 await their next duties at Tonghua shed, November 1997. AF

JS6366 pulls out of Hunjiang yard with a northbound freight, January 2001. GE

Last rites for China Rail steam

The demands on the national rail system, China Rail, are enormous, and passenger numbers and freight tonnages have been rising almost continually for many years. Unlike the UK or the USA, where the majority of railway lines were constructed in the 19th century, a significant number of lines in China were built in the second half of the 20th century and new lines are still being constructed today. At the same time existing lines are being upgraded and other measures taken to increase capacity. Such measures have included a general speeding up of all trains, and running longer and heavier trains. By the mid 1980s it was apparent that China's existing classes of steam locomotive were not capable of achieving these objectives and the decision was made to phase out steam. The express passenger steam locomotives of the SL and RM classes were unable to cope with the longer and heavier trains and all were withdrawn by 1991. Surprisingly, QJ and JS class locomotives continued to be built for China Rail until December 1988 and these were the last steam classes to run on the main lines.

We were too late - railway enthusiasts are always too late. Wherever they go in search of steam and whatever they find, they always lament not having been there earlier, before an earlier class of loco had been withdrawn, before the infrastructure had been modernised, or before the line had been dieselised. And so it was with our visits. By the time of our first visits in 1997, the overwhelming majority of the national network had been dieselised or electrified. The remaining steam operations were mostly confined to a few secondary and branch lines. Even in the late 1980s large cities like Changchun and Harbin in the north-east still had substantial allocations of steam locos. At Changchun an average of a steam-hauled movement every six minutes throughout the day had been reported. Harbin was famous for Sankong yard, a large freight marshalling yard with a road overbridge at one end. From this bridge double-headed QJs could be observed making spectacular departures with heavy freights. Out in the west, the China Rail main line near Zhongwei was a mecca for enthusiasts with its long winding climb through harsh but impressive scenery.

But we were too late – by the time we got to China, all this was over. During the mid to late 1990s, China Rail's workshops were turning out around 1000 diesel and electric locomotives annually. At the same time an economic slowdown eased the pressure on the railways a little, allowing large inroads to be made in the steam locomotive fleet. Mercifully, from our point of view, a number of pockets with steam remained. Amongst others, there was Baotou - with its JS-hauled 13-coach suburban trains and the nearby scenic Shiguai branch, Yebaishou – where three lines diverged, each with lengthy climbs through hills, Fuxin - an important freight

View from the cab of QJ 6892 on its way from Nancha to Yichun, March 1997. AF

route with a regular procession of QJ-hauled freights, and the Pinglou to Rujigou branch - with very dramatic scenery but in a restricted area, meaning few foreign visitors made it there. Fortunately for John, he did. One by one these steam outposts disappeared and by early 2002 the network was free of steam traction, with the exception of the Wuhai to Jilantai branch in Inner Mongolia, which lasted into 2003.

Nancha, some 350 kilometres north-east of Harbin in Heilongjiang province offered some of the most spectacular sights of steam locomotives hard at work in the whole of China. All-out efforts were required by the locomotives and crews to get their trains up the bank and over the summit just north of Nancha on the Wuyiling branch. Double heading and the use of a banking engine were the norm, particularly for the heavy southbound freights, often timber from the extensive forestry operations further north. By the time we got there in 1997, operations were somewhat blighted by diesel locomotives piloting and banking many of the freights.

It was often the case that the quality of steam railway activity in an area was inversely proportional to the quality of the hotels, and the hotel at Nancha was clearly under the impression that steam still reigned supreme on Nancha bank. For the second evening in the hotel, hot water had been promised in the communal wash and shower room between 8 and 9 pm. Having missed out on a shower the previous night and with the night before that being spent on a sleeper train, Gordon and Adrian were keen to have a clean up and therefore duly presented themselves in the shower room at the allotted hour. "Meiyou" - cold water only. Ah, but perhaps all was not lost. What was this helpful hotel assistant doing? He had produced two battered enamel bowls, taken them over to the radiator on the wall and was fiddling about with a piece of plastic hose attached to the central heating pipework. Moments later hot, pungent-smelling, brownish water was filling the bowls. The assistant gesticulated to our shower-hopefuls to stand up and tip the bowl's contents over their heads. Well, obviously! So as an alternative to a clean-up, the layer of dirt and dust was replaced with a layer of rust. Oh well, only two more days until the next hotel.

A light load for JS8322 leaving Shiguai with coal for Baotou, March 1999. JT

Decorations adorn the cabside of QJ 6484 at Da'an Bei, March 2000. AF

QJ6726 climbs into Yebaishou with a freight from the north-east, February 1998. JT

24

Early morning activity at Bei'an station, March 1999. JT

QJ 6547 approaches Dawukou from Pingluo with coal empties, February 1998. JT

QJ 6547 climbs into the hills above Linshugou with empties for Rujigou, February 1998. JT

QJ 6749 near Linshugou with the daily passenger to Rujigou, February 1998. JT

QJ 6127 approaching Dadenggou with the daily
passenger to Rujigou, February 1998. JT

(next page) JS 8279 accelerates from Baotou Xi station on a
morning Baotou circle line suburban train, October 1998. AF

An unidentified QJ leaves Jiamusi with a freight towards Boli during the dying days of steam in the area, February 1999. JT

(right) QJ 6617 approaching Zaowo and facing the long climb into the hills towards Rujigou, February 1998. JT

Liushu, on the Nancha to Wuyiling line, is host to an unidentified northbound QJ, March 1997. GE

JS 6468 shunts at a permanent way yard at Shenyang Huanggutun, November 1997. AF

High-deflector QJ 3257 pulls out of Bei'an yard with a freight for Qiqihar, March 1999. JT

QJ 6752 on the long haul out of Fuxin with a freight for Shenyang, February 1998. JT

QJ 3344 climbs to the summit west of Yebaishou on the Chengde line, November 1997. AF

Heilongjiang coal systems

China is the world's largest consumer of coal and it has more coal deposits than any other country apart from the USA. Coal was being burned in China centuries before its discovery by western nations. Marco Polo described coal in his books of travel in China, where he saw it used in houses for cooking and heating, but not knowing what it was he referred to it as 'black stones'.

In 2000, China produced 1 billion tonnes of coal; by 2006 this figure had more than doubled to 2.3 billion and it is expected to rise more gradually to 2.6 billion by 2010. China's rapid economic growth has been fuelled by coal, and it accounts for approximately three-quarters of the country's energy needs. As the demand for energy increases, it has been forecast that 500 new coal-fired power stations will be built in the next ten years – nearly one a week.

There are five million miners in China but safety in coal mines has a poor record. There were more than 4700 deaths in mining accidents in 2006, a dreadful figure but the lowest for 30 years. The majority of these deaths happened in small mines – those with an annual production below 30 000 tonnes - and there is an active programme to close many of these mines down. Although primitive and the sort of thing that disappeared in most Western countries over 100 years ago, many of these small mines only date from the 1980s, when the Chinese economy took off and the number mushroomed to around 80 000. There are estimated to be 24 000 today and the target is to reduce this number to 10 000 by 2010, but despite the regulations, numerous new small operations are being set up and it is doubtful whether the target will be met.

Heilongjiang is the most north-easterly province in China and borders Russia. It is characterised by long and extremely cold winters, and it is rare for the temperature to rise anywhere near freezing point for the whole of January. This province has several large coal mining areas, three of which are at Hegang, Shuangyashan and Jixi. All have extensive railway systems and continued to make use of steam locomotives after they had finished on China Rail.

At Jixi, 570 kilometres east of the provincial capital of Harbin, a number of separate railway systems served a collection of mines. They were exclusively operated by SY class locomotives until the arrival of diesels in 2007.

Approximately 150 kilometres due north of Jixi lay Shuangyashan at the end of a short China Rail branch. The mine railway began here where China Rail ended and continued for some 70 kilometres. In addition to the coal traffic, passenger services were run along this line and three branches. Its use of QJ class locomotives to perform these duties gave the system a 'main line' feel although a few SY class were also deployed for shunting, trip working and lighter tasks. Inconveniently, the passenger trains did not start at the China Rail station, but at the system's own station, approximately two kilometres distant. At Shuangyashan we first saw

An SY moves off Baicheng washery on the Chengzihe mining system, Jixi, January 2007. AF

outside stalls selling ice lollies simply laid out on tables, there being no danger of them melting.

Gordon and Adrian travelled hard sleeper from Harbin to Shuangyashan in December 2000. It is probable that some of the other passengers were unaccustomed to seeing Westerners, or as they would call them, 'big noses'. During the hour or so before lights went out the joker in the group of six sleeper berths primed them with dried fish slices and beer from the refreshment trolley before doing his best to embarrass Gordon. He found the size of Gordon's nose of infinite amusement and so amazed was this man of Gordon's projection, that he would regularly grab hold of it as if to test whether it was real, before whooping with delight and inviting the other passengers to join in. Fortunately for Gordon, the lights were turned out in the sleeper coach at 10 p.m. bringing to an abrupt end this test in tolerance.

Furthest north of these three mining areas and approximately 70 kilometres from the Russian border, lies Hegang, where coal mining began in 1916. Hegang is an important coal mining city with reserves of 3 billion tonnes, although much of its appearance belies this fact. It is a cosmopolitan city with a population of over brushes, shovelled into sacks and then wheeled away, two or three sacks being balanced on a bicycle crossbar. So much sweeping has occurred at certain track sections that the ballast has also been brushed away and the sleepers supporting the rails were partially undermined. Elsewhere on the railway, blatant coal theft was rife with coal shovelled out of loaded wagons in broad daylight.

The system's lines radiated from the central exchange yard with China Rail. Most of the lines had overhead electric wires at 1500V d.c. and a fleet of electric locomotives handled the majority of the coal traffic. This left passenger workings on two lines, spoil trains from the various mines and miscellaneous workings to be handled by the fleet of SYs. There were large numbers of small mines in the Hegang area, but with each of the four visits made between 2001 and 2007, the numbers of these have visibly declined. Although looking a little run down on the first couple of visits, recent expansion of some of the large mines and the decision to purchase diesel locomotives suggests the operation has a healthy balance sheet.

SY 3014 on a spoil train at Xing'an, Hegang, January 2005. AF

one million. Much of it is laid out on a grand scale with wide boulevards flanked by tall buildings. Many new apartment blocks have been constructed recently and, externally at least, look quite smart.

The city clearly wishes to present an image of prosperity to visitors. To this end, crass and tasteless artefacts of municipal pride adorn the main thoroughfares. Street lighting comprises of elaborate lamp posts each supporting clusters of 30 – 40 lamps. At major junctions, traffic islands are home to large sculptures. A copy of the Arc de Triomphe has been constructed at the side of the main road into town. Garishly illuminated plastic palm trees abound and a selection of replica dinosaurs stands outside a civic building. A toilet block outside the main railway station has been built in the style of a medieval castle.

Contrasting this were large areas of single-storey hutons offering basic accommodation for their occupants, although many of the hutons are being cleared away. Smog in these districts could be dreadful. Evidence by railway lines close to the hutons suggested that the communal toilet blocks were woefully inadequate. Along the railway tracks and especially where the coal wagons were shunted, scores of coal scavengers recovered the fragments of coal that had fallen out of the wagons. In places this activity had almost reached industrial scale. As empty wagons were shunted, shovels rained on the wagon doors and underframes to dislodge any remaining coal. This was rapidly swept into mounds with twig

Beichang washery and coal slurry settling beds, Chengzihe mining system, Jixi, January 2006. JT

QJ 6805 departs Zhongxin for Shuangxing on the Shuangyashan mine railway, January 2002. JT

View from a spoil heap of Dalu mine, Hegang, as an unidentified SY slips past in the background, January 2002. GE

Dusk at Fuli. An SY shunts wagons in a factory siding. Hegang, January 2004. AF

SY 1464 on passenger train 4 from Junli to Hegang, near Dalu, January 2005. AF

SY 0498 at Nanshan mine on spoil, Hegang, January 2004. AF   (next page) SY on the morning Xingshan to Hegang passenger train at Liucao, January 2005. AF

The afternoon passenger near Dalu as it makes its way from Junli to Hegang behind SY1498, January 2002. GE

Nanchang loco servicing point on the Chengzihe mining system, Jixi, Christmas Day 2006. AF

Digging out partially solidified coal slurry from the settling beds by Baichang washery, Chengzihe mining system, Jixi, January 2006. JT

Miners available for hire, Hegang, January 2002. AF

A coal scavenger takes a break. Hegang shed, November 2005. GE

Dislodging scraps of coal during shunting. Hegang, January 2005. JT

Sacks of scavenged coal are wheeled away. Hegang, January 2005. JT

An unidentified SY runs light engine through the morning mist at Beichang on the Chengzihe mining system, Jixi, January 2006. JT

Low afternoon sun illuminates the exchange yard at Hengshan mining system, Jixi, March 1999. JT

QJ 6805 passes the outskirts of Shuangyashan on New Year's Eve 2001 on the last run of train 21 to Dongbaowei.
Service reductions took place the following day, eliminating this working. AF

QJ3598 approaches Dongjing with a Fushan train. Shuangyashan, January 2002. GE

A lone SY passes abandoned small mines at Dalu on the Hegang system, January 2002. AF

Locomotives, sheds and workshops

The construction of steam locomotives for China Rail finished in December 1988, when the final batches of QJ and JS class were outshopped from Datong works, some 370 kilometres west of Beijing. Datong then switched over to the construction of diesels for China Rail. Production of SY class for industry continued intermittently until 1999, mostly at Tangshan works, but a small number were also built at Changchun in 1998/9. These represent two world 'lasts' – the last steam locomotives to be built for main line use and the last steam locomotives to be built for commercial use. A number of the newer locomotives saw less than ten years of service before withdrawal. SY 3023 and 3024, Changchun's most recent, went to Hegang coal mine railway but the latter engine only saw about six years' service before being taken out of use. The world's newest loco, SY 1772, completed at Tangshan in October 1999, is believed to be still in normal service at the Tiefa mining railway in Liaoning province at the time of writing.

The locomotive classifications are abbreviations of the pinyin names and translate roughly as follows:

前进 Qian Jin = QJ or 'progress' or perhaps 'march forward'
建设 Jian She = JS or 'construction'
上游 Shang You = SY or 'aiming high'

Chinese steam locomotive design was heavily influenced by American, Russian and Japanese practise.

The large QJ class 2-10-2s were the standard freight locomotives and over 4700 were built between 1971 and 1988. Many were also used on passenger duties including a number of express and long distance trains. Complete with tender, they weighed some 250 tonnes. Many of the QJs were fitted with mechanical stokers, but these were often not used in order to save coal. Locomotive crews used to receive bonuses based on the amount of coal they could save.

The smaller JS class 2-8-2s were designed for branch line work, shunting and short freight duties. Its design dates back to the 1950s and 1900 were built in two main batches, one from 1957 to 1965, then after a long gap, again from 1981 to 1988. This latter batch was constructed to replace a number of older, non-standard designs.

Over 1800 of the standard industrial locomotive design, the SY class 2-8-2s, were built between 1960 and 1999. These form the majority of the surviving steam locomotives in China today.

Certain locomotives of each class received adornments or decorations, which may have been as simple as brass numbers or numberplates attached to each cab side instead of the usual painted numbers, but sometimes extended to brass boiler

Bitterly cold work for the shunter at Daban depot, January 2004. JT

bands and slogans around the smokebox. Such slogans usually either encouraged hard work or promoted safety. At the time of writing, a few of the SYs still in service retain their decorations.

Chinese steam locomotives had a crew of three – a driver, an assistant driver and a fireman. Firing the locos was hard work and this job was shared with the assistant driver, who doubled up as a second fireman.

Even after the complete withdrawal of steam locomotives from China Rail, a few workshops continued to overhaul locomotives belonging to industrial and local railways. However, China Rail began to impose restrictions on steam locomotives moving over their tracks, and this made it difficult for some industrial users to get their locomotives to the works. Mudanjiang Steam Locomotive Workshop was the last of the China Rail workshops to carry out overhauls, and closed in July 2005. Many of the QJs that worked on the JiTong local railway had been overhauled here. Some industrial users were capable of doing their own heavy overhauls, such as Pingdingshan, Anshan and Jalainur.

Conditions inside sheds and workshops were usually rather primitive, but most industrial users provided no undercover accommodation for their working fleet at

Hegang shed with SY1498 on the left, November 2005. GE

QJ 6111 takes coal at Jiamusi depot, February 1999. JT

all. Locomotive preparation such as oiling the motion, filling the sand dome, raking out the ash and watering was carried out in the open all year round. At stabling points on industrial systems, ash pickers – scavengers searching for fragments of unburned coal through the discarded ash from the locomotives' fireboxes – were often to be found with the tools of their trade, hand rakes, trowels, brushes and sacks. If the going was good, a bicycle would be needed so the laden sack could be balanced over the crossbar and wheeled away.

There was often a blow down area at a stabling point. Blowing down involved clearing the sludge from the bottom of the boiler and needed to be carried out regularly. A mixture of water, steam and sludge was ejected from the side of the loco and produced a huge cloud of steam. Fixed screens to shield off this activity were provided if this was done near a road of public access. In the north during winter all this water and steam would freeze and gangs of ice-breakers were deployed with pickaxes to break up and remove the build-up of ice.

Despite the large number of steam locomotives that have been withdrawn from service in recent times, it is unlikely that they will languish around for long before being cut up, given China's terrific demand for steel. The country has a few railway museums, but China is not a sentimental nation and looks to the future rather than the past. Most Chinese don't care that steam is disappearing and are totally bemused by Western railway enthusiasts' interest in what they regard as the old fashioned and outdated.

The final weeks of JS activity at Chaoyangchuan shed, October 1998. AF

QJ's 6903, 2823 and 6792 at Yichun shed, March 1997. GE

SY 0837 undergoes repair in the workshops at Anshan steelworks, February 1998. JT

JS 8122 receives a major overhaul at Pingdingshan workshops with JS 6429 behind, January 2003. AF

A QJ boiler receives attention at Changchun works, October 1998. AE

QJ 6981 awaits the next turn of duty as night falls on Jixi depot, March 1999. JT

Line-up at Chang'an workshops, Shuangyashan, comprising SY 1045 and QJs 6806, 7019 and 3594, December 2000. GE

JS 8223 receives attention at Gusheng workshops, Hekounan, November 2005. GE

Loco preparation, Xiamiaozi stabling point, Nanpiao, January 2004. AF

Shovelling ash at Huludao, December 2004. AF

Steam cleaning SY wheels at Dongchang, Jixi, January 2007. AF

Shuangyashan stabling point sand filler with QJ7020, New Year's Day 2001. GE

SY 1102, QJ 6806 and QJ 3594 at Shuangyashan stabling point, January 2002. GE

QJ 6904 on Jixi depot at sunrise, March 1999. JT

JS 8057 on Pingdingshan shed, October 2003. AF

Southern China

Whereas most of our visits to China have taken us to the bitter cold of the north-east in winter, where people would only venture outdoors if wrapped up like mummies, things were very different in southern China. For a start, it was green! And how pleasant it was to be able to change films without the fingers risking frostbite.

There were fewer surviving steam lines in Southern China, but amongst these were some real gems. Pride of place went to a narrow gauge line known as Shibanxi, south of Chengdu in Sichuan province. Under threat of closure for several years, it has recently been promoted by the Chinese as a tourist line. It was built to carry coal from the mine to a power station and was not connected to any other railways. This line had the advantage that the main town it served – Bagou - had no road access, meaning that everything not produced locally needed to be brought in by train and so the passenger trains also carried all manner of goods. An illustration of this reliance on the railway was the sight of a woman laying on a stretcher at a station waiting for the next service train to evacuate her to hospital.

The service used rather basic coaches built in the railway's own workshop. These vehicles had a wooden bench along each side, they were unlit and had no glass in the windows. The only brakes were manually applied via a handwheel in each coach. Every coach had its own conductor who collected the fares and wound the handwheel on or off at stations and on gradients. These were usually women, whose sole concession to a uniform was wearing a pink hat.

If catching the first train of the day during winter, the journey would mostly be spent in complete darkness and the conductors were issued with torches so that fares could still be taken. Periodically, glowing embers dropped by the locomotive could be glimpsed on the track through the gaps in the coach floorboards and when going through the tunnels, steam and sparks would swirl into the coach through the unglazed windows.

All the coaches were frequently laden with goods, but the centre coach was longer than the others and was officially designated for goods, and particularly livestock, which usually meant pigs. For this purpose a section at the end was penned off. The timetable did not allow for the variable duration of the stops needed to load or unload goods or the pigs, who could be quarrelsome and uncooperative. Pigs were frequent travellers, though presumably only once, and then only one way. Fare for a pig was 10 Yuan as against 5 Yuan for locals or 30 Yuan for tourists.

On one occasion the last train of the day was especially crowded. A farmer wanted to load several pigs into the pen but it was already occupied by a young buffalo. (The loading must have been an interesting spectacle, since everything had to be manhandled in from track level.) The farmer was insistent that his pigs should be allowed on, so all the passengers waited patiently as long heated

A home-made trolley is deployed to move the vegetables, Shibanxi, October 2003. GE

discussions took place outside. The problem was finally solved by the simple solution of emptying all the passengers out of one of the smaller coaches and putting the pigs in their place.

Buffalo are a common sight working in the fields across China; these domesticated animals are apparently placid enough to be in the care of sometimes very young children, and show few of the traits of their wild African cousins. Just occasionally, however, their wilder side shows itself. One morning, just at first light, the first train of the day was thrashing uphill towards the horseshoe curve, when it suddenly came to a shuddering halt. Heads appeared at all the windows and the bleary-eyed passengers peered forward into the gloom. Ahead was a large buffalo, not just blocking the line but positively scowling at the train and threatening to charge should the train have the temerity to challenge it by moving forward another pace. Again a long delay ensued with the passengers waiting patiently, until the buffalo was finally coaxed to the side of the track where it could be tethered to a tree.

Bricks required for any building work would be brought on the train – in the goods coach if the quantity needed was small or on a wagon of their own if more were required. Offloading them from a wagon was simple – they were tipped into a heap, many being broken in the process, and they would be moved to their destination by horses with panniers. December was timber and bamboo season. Logs were brought to the nearest railhead by horse, bamboo by human. Substantial loads of bamboo were carried, cut to approximately three-metre lengths and strapped across the top of a basket on the carrier's back. Special trains ran to handle this seasonal traffic.

A small coal mine at Huangcunjin, the line's terminus, produced sufficient output for one or two trains a day. Miners pushed small tubs on 300mm gauge rails in and out of the mine, which made a horizontal entry into the side of a hill. Emptying a tub involved tipping it on its side using a wooden pit prop as a lever. This mine closed in 2004, but a new mine has been opened with dual gauge track, using some of the original tubs and some larger 600mm gauge tubs, also pushed by hand.

Down by the station at Huangcunjin was a building with what looked like graffiti on it. The graffiti was official and warned people that it was illegal to have more than one child, or to have a child when under the age of 20. The penalty was 17 000 Yuan, an unaffordable sum for low paid villagers. Having a third child would incur a further penalty of 22 000 Yuan.

East of Shibanxi, another narrow gauge line was isolated from the main railway network. The Weiyuan Coal Railway was eight kilometres long and built to carry coal from Huangjinggou to a cement factory. Although it once ran a passenger service, in recent years there was usually only a single out-and-back coal working per day, and that was early in the morning. In the town of Huangjinggou the line ran down the high street, where a daily market was held. The outward journey was before the market had been set up but the return was when it was in full swing and traders had to move baskets of satsumas, apples and bananas out of the way to allow the train to creep past.

The Chenzhou narrow gauge in Hunan province was a remarkable line. Only opened in 1985 to serve coal mines at Jiahe, it was built to main line standards with bridges, cuttings, embankments and large graceful viaducts. Whether the investment ever paid off is questionable since the line closed within 20 years. Geological difficulties reduced the output of the mine to a trickle and the line was finally seen off by serious flood damage. When we visited in November 2001, only one return working remained, run as a mixed train with a passenger coach, covered wagon and coal wagons if required. The train was chiefly used by traders on their way to the market at Guiyang, the main stop on the route. An incredible number of market gardeners, complete with vegetables and sugar cane, managed to cram themselves into the single covered wagon for this journey.

A few isolated standard gauge outposts held on to steam into the beginning of this century such as the Datong Coal Railway, Hechi, where the route passed through the classic limestone Karst mountain scenery, and Pingshi, not far from Chenzhou.

Travelling from Hechi on the overnight train from Liuzhou to Hengshan

and then on to Chenzhou, Adrian was persuaded to make a purchase from the refreshment trolley. His choice? Rather obvious really – 'Paddy Flower Sparrow Tonic Wine', which described itself thus: "Having been removed fat and fishy by unique methode and carefully well-compounded storage for a year, Paddy Flower Sparrow Tonic Wine is mainly made by adapting paddy flower sparrow and combined with astralagus membranaceus, lycium chinese, angcliiea sinensis, polygonatum sibiricum and longan pulp, etc for more than twenties rare medicinal herds which is made with pure rice wine for half a year. The wine looks dark brown and bright clearness. It contains 36 per cent alcohol. A little sweet but not chilly, coordinated sparrow drugs, sweet wine and smell. It smells good and flavour. With the functions of nourishing the blood and reinforcing ones vitality. It fits to weak in body and pain in kidney, also man and woman to drink in seasons." Well, none of your attractive bouquet, balanced oak flavours and soft fruitiness nonsense, this was evidently the real product. What the label didn't make clear was whether the "weak in body and pain in kidney" bit was expected to occur before or after drinking, but upon sampling, the latter seemed far more probable.

Bamboo on the move, Shibanxi, December 2006. AF

The fourth and last train of the day at Shibanxi climbs round the big horseshoe curve, May 2004. JT

Supervisors watch on as ore is loaded at Xiaoyutou on the Datong coal railway, May 2004. JT

JS 8287 waits at Wenping for a southbound freight to cross. Hechi, November 2001. AF

Night is closing in as a team of labourers set about loading coal wagons by hand at Xiaoyutou on the Datong coal railway, May 2004. JT

Tea time. JS 8287 at Wenping, Hechi, November 2001. AF

A miner waits with his loaded tub for the coal tipping area to be vacated, Huangcunjin, Shibanxi, October 2003. AF

Even ladies shovel coal, October 2003. AF

Cigarette break, October 2003. AF

A loaded tub emerges from the mine at Huangcunjin, October 2003. GE

Returning for more, October 2003. GE

JS 8287 heads north through Karst hills at Neitun. Hechi, November 2001. AF

Pingdingshan and Central China

Xi'an, famed for its terracotta warriors, and Zhengzhou, a major textile base, are the two largest cities in central China. Between these two, a small number of industrial railways hung on to steam. By far the largest of these was the system linking several coal mines at Pingdingshan. Two narrow gauge lines survived with steam: Yinghao linked a coal mine with China Rail and immediately west of Zhengzhou was a brickworks line at Xingyang. Metre-gauge lines were unusual in China but further north-east at Xihe near Zibo, one such line remained until 2000. Central China doesn't suffer the extreme cold conditions of the north-east during winter, but it does get occasional snow falls and overnight frosts are common.

The success of Pingdingshan, a city of one million inhabitants, was built on coal. Although the centre was quite cosmopolitan, like many Chinese cities the air could be very polluted, and coal dust was never far away. A visit, made a few years ago during October, when it rained continually for the duration, found the city's outer edges had turned to quagmires formed of dirt and coal dust. However, Pingdingshan has been changing, with whole districts being demolished, roads widened and new flyovers and underpasses constructed. The railway has also done well with infrastructure upgrading and capacity increases. Several coal mines are linked by an extensive system of lines. A connection with China Rail allows empty wagons to be brought onto the system and loads to be taken away via the national network. The two main routes on this system have passenger services, which can be used by the public. Until 2004, the system exclusively deployed steam traction but since then several diesels have been purchased. The railway has its own workshops and could perform heavy overhauls on its fleet of steam locomotives, which comprise all three standard locomotive types – SY, JS and QJ, although the arrival of diesels relegated the QJs to standby duties.

For such a large city, Pingdingshan was poorly served by China Rail trains and the few there were tended to be very full. Although happy to spend two weeks at Pingdingshan, the time came to leave. We wanted to take an overnight train to Handan, but had great difficulty getting any tickets and managed only unreserved hard seats. By the time we got to the station for the 00:38 departure, there was already a huge crowd, mostly of young people all waiting for this train, and we expected a grim night in an overfull coach. Unusually, we and the other passengers were allowed onto the platform before the train had arrived and when it rolled in the crowd of passengers cheered since it was clear that there were plenty of free hard seats. Attempting to board the train was the inevitable scrum which invariably saw 'big noses' boarding last, but an official checked our tickets and directed us to the coach with an upgrade desk. It emerged that both soft

Making popcorn at Dakunlun, Xihe, November 1999. GE

and hard sleeper upgrades were available so we went soft for 12 Yuan each (in addition to the original 53 Yuan ticket) and had an unexpectedly comfortable journey. Overnights on the move weren't always as agreeable!

As is the case elsewhere in China, narrow gauge operations could be rather hit and miss and the Xingyang brickworks line was more hit and miss than most. The line took clay from a clay pit to the brickworks and was frequently out of use due to wet weather preventing the clay being dug, overproduction/insufficient sales, breakdown or holidays. In recent years, Xingyang high street contrasted starkly with this backward operation with numerous up-market retailers – outlets for electric bicycles and wedding dress shops being particularly well represented.

By the time of closure, the metre gauge line from Dakunlun on the China Rail system to the coal mine at Xihe was unique. Ten-coupled engines hauled empties up to Xihe on a severely graded line, on which the train often moved at little more than walking pace and usually had to stop a couple of times to get up sufficient steam pressure to proceed. The downhill return with the loaded coal wagons was somewhat easier. Towards the end of the line's existence these engines leaked so much steam that in cold conditions engine and train were sometimes completely engulfed in the exhaust.

In Dakunlun, we came across our first Chinese popcorn street vendor, although it was initially far from clear what his equipment was for. Corn for popping and a magic ingredient were put in a cylindrical steel vessel with a lid, which was sealed closed with a heavy duty quick release latch. This was mounted

JS5644 leaves Pingdingshan on empties, January 2003. GE

in a framework with a handle so it could be rotated. A fire of coal dust burned beneath the vessel whilst it was turned so that it heated up evenly, and a gauge displayed the internal pressure. After ten minutes of handle turning, the pressure had built up sufficiently and the vessel was removed from the flames and put into a large mesh tube. A crowbar was used to release the latch and the lid shot open with a bang emitting a huge cloud of steam. When the steam had disappeared the tube was full of popcorn, which could be emptied into a basket. And the magic ingredient? The vendor spat into the vessel before closing the lid!

Loading cattle at Sipo, south of Pingdingshan, January 2003. GE

Lady crossing keeper, Pingdingshan, October 2003. GE

A lack of activity at Xingyang, September 2003. AF

(next page) SY 1417 heads for Sipo, January 2003. GE

Redundant C4 class at Xuchang, October 2003. AF

JS 5644 by the coking plant at Pingdingshan, January 2003. GE

Capes and cycles in the Pingdingshan rain, October 2003. AF

Coal empties from Dakunlun climb towards the mine on the metre-gauge Xihe mine railway, November 1999. GE

SY 0758 passes 7th Mine at Pingdingshan with the morning passenger train to Hanzhuang, October 2003. AF

View from a defunct spoil heap with an unidentified QJ taking empties to 4th Mine, Pingdingshan, January 2003. AF

Coal empties approach Xihe, November 1999. GE

SY 1002 at Lingwazhen level crossing on the afternoon train to Baofeng and Hanzhuang. Pingdingshan, October 2003. GE

Exceptional levels of smog at Pingdingshan as QJ 6450 lifts empties out of Tianzhuang yard, January 2003. AF

Trains, stations, tickets and the occasional bus

Most long distance travel in China is done by train and passenger numbers grow every year. The Chinese pattern of running passenger trains is rather different from that of the UK. Instead of numerous short trains shuttling between centres at frequent service intervals, Chinese trains are less frequent but much longer and most cover much greater distances. Many long distance trains take more than 24 hours to get from start to finish and some more than two days. One effect of this is that arrivals and departures from stations on the way can be at strange hours during the day or night. A benefit of having fewer but longer trains is that it helps maximise track capacity for the all-important freight traffic.

Stations, particularly in large towns and cities, are enormous, and can be rather daunting for the traveller who doesn't speak Chinese. The first problem is working out where to buy the tickets. Following the throng into the station is no use without one, since the ticket office is usually either in a different part of the station or in a different building altogether. Saying "shòu piào chù" to someone would get you pointed in the right direction. Buying tickets could vary from being dead easy to downright impossible.

Although John launched into his early solo trips prepared to struggle along mostly by using luck, this method was considered totally unsatisfactory by the others. Adrian had a slip of paper with the basic ticket request written on it, with blank spaces where the destination, date, train time and number and the type of ticket (hard seat, hard sleeper, soft sleeper) could be inserted. The slip was photocopied sufficient times for the whole trip to China, filled out using the appropriate Chinese characters for the destination and ticket type, and passed to the clerk at the ticket counter. It usually worked and if attempted a few days in advance of the journey, the success rate would be much higher. Of course upon seeing the request, the ticket clerk would reasonably assume that we could read Chinese and a response, unintelligible to us, was sometimes written on the slip and handed back. Well intentioned no doubt, but not very useful. It was very rare to encounter anyone in the ticket office that spoke any English. Where possible, long journeys were made overnight to minimise loss of useful daylight hours and on these trips we would attempt to buy hard sleeper berths. If that failed, it would be hard seats, with the hope of being able to upgrade to hard sleeper once on the train.

John recalls the following experience trying to get tickets at Jixi: "A local university student had been thrilled to meet me and have a chance to practise his English. I planned to leave Jixi on an overnight sleeper, so I enlisted the help of my new friend to purchase my ticket. We tried on each of three days prior to my intended departure, and each time they refused to sell us a ticket, without

Dual language signs in part of the vast concourse at Harbin station, January 2005. JT

explanation, or at least not one that was translated to me. Come the day of my departure, he suggested to me that I buy a hard seat ticket and try for an upgrade on the train, but I really wanted the assurance of a sleeper ticket before I got aboard. 'Then the only thing is to try to buy a private ticket', he said. With no idea what he was talking about, I trailed back again to the station. He did not go to the ticket window this time, but to a woman manning one of the telephone booths. She demanded 150 Yuan, which I handed over, and she then went to the same ticket window where we had been rebuffed, and was given a ticket without question. The ticket showed the 'correct' price of 64 Yuan. My student was somewhat embarrassed by the whole episode, but forestalled any thought I might have had about complaining by pointing out that the railway police would also be taking their cut out of the profit."

The Chinese system is all about control. Although a station may be huge, there is always only one set of doors open to let people in and police are present to ensure that everyone puts their bags on to the conveyor for an X-ray machine at the entrance. This was a constant annoyance for us with our film. A few years ago it was generally easy to bypass the X-ray machines simply by walking straight past them, although if we showed this disrespect when travelling with a guide, they panicked and immediately disowned us. Now the police have become more thorough and it has become impossible to get away with that, but so far the film has always managed to evade these machines.

Inside, a smaller station would have a single large waiting hall at ground level;

has its own policeman. After departure, the conductor comes along with a book of tokens and exchanges the tickets for these tokens. This allows the conductor to see where each passenger is going to and about half an hour before arrival time, the conductor will rouse the appropriate passengers, swap the token back for the ticket and make sure they are ready to get off. Flasks of boiling water are provided in the coaches – the Chinese use it to top up their jars or flasks of green tea, we occasionally used it for tea, coffee or soups that we had brought with us. Although all coaches have displayed 'no smoking' signs for many years, it has only been enforced in recent times, smoking being confined to the vestibules at each end of the coach, and only encountered when a visit to the toilet became necessary. Hard class toilets are of the 'squat' variety, discharging directly onto the track below and for some inexplicable reason, the toilets are often heated to furnace-like temperatures.

From about 7 o'clock in the morning, music is played over the coach p.a. system. On our earlier journeys, this was Chinese music, a favourite being 'Butterfly Lovers', the musical interpretation of a Chinese legend about a tragic romance between two lovers. Sadly this has largely been replaced with versions of popular Western music and a more recent trip included an instrumental rendering of the Commodores' 'Three times a lady' and the 'Titanic' film theme tune. On disembarking, any tranquillity and civility in the coach interior vanishes abruptly and the chaotic reality of the outside world returns, especially once through the station barriers, when the amassed pack of taxi drivers spot and home in on potential premium-rate passengers amongst the new arrivals.

Sleeper buses are an alternative to overnights on the train, and are cheaper, if not necessarily more comfortable, as Adrian and Gordon found out in January 2001. "Gordon and I were heading back to Beijing from Hunjiang to catch our flight home. A direct train from Hunjiang deposited us at Shenyang Bei station at 17:38, where, according to the timetable, we could choose between four overnight trains that would get us in to Beijing in plenty of time for the following day's late morning flight departure. The station ticket hall was packed. Large digital displays above the ticket counters indicated the availability of tickets for soft sleeper, hard sleeper and hard seats on the major long distance trains for the next two weeks. Watching this information scroll through, it became apparent that all the trains we thought we could have caught were fully booked for the next eight days. The slip of paper with the train details written down would be no help. Over the last two and a half weeks of travelling, we had never had a problem getting tickets for the trains we wanted and naively assumed that this journey would be no different, so we were at a bit of a loss what to do now. The lady tugging my arm knew exactly what to do. Jabbering and gesticulating, then pulling the slip of paper out of my hand and writing reams of doubtless useful, but unintelligible, script on it we slowly worked out what she was explaining. There was a bus bound for Beijing in the station forecourt. But when would it leave and could it get to Beijing as quickly as the train? The distance was over 700 kilometres and the roads were all covered in compacted snow. Would we make in time for our

Beijing station, March 2000. AF

in larger stations waiting halls are on the first floor. Knowing your train number is essential in order to find the appropriate waiting hall or section within the hall. Passengers are never allowed straight onto the platforms but must wait here until the train is announced, by which time the waiting hall is invariably packed. A scrum frequently ensues as everyone pushes forward, through the crowd control barriers and to the ticket inspector before being allowed onto the platform. Soft sleeper ticket holders have some advantages – a separate, more comfortable waiting room and priority boarding. The long distance trains can easily have 16 coaches or more, so it can be quite a walk to get to the right coach. Although the coaches have a door at each end, only one is opened for boarding, the other remaining permanently locked. Each coach has a conductor (a 'dragon lady'), who stands at the door and checks the tickets again before boarding is permitted.

Once the hassle of buying tickets and entering the station, and the mayhem of the waiting room, ticket inspection and train boarding were over, the sleeper berths located, luggage stowed away, some of the excess layers removed and the train had set off, it was possible to relax with a beer from the refreshment trolley and reflect on the day's events.

Hard sleepers are perfectly adequate for an overnight journey, the only disadvantage with them is that there is an open corridor down one side of the coach, so security is not as good as soft sleepers, with their closed compartments and a bit more space. However, crime levels are low and with each coach having its own conductor, security is unlikely to be an issue; additionally every train in China

flights? We were shown into the bus - a sleeper bus, no less - with a mix of sleeping berths down one side, and seating down the other. It was a pleasant surprise. The outside temperature was well below -25°C, but a brazier was keeping the bus nice and warm. The berths were wider than I expected. We bought our tickets for a reasonable 150 Yuan each and loaded our bags in. Ah, first misconception: each 'berth' was actually meant for two, not one as we had imagined. We bought bottles of water for the journey and sat and waited for the stated 20:00 departure. The agreeable temperature inside the bus enticed us, rather rashly, to remove various layers of thermals. Second misconception: that we would depart at the specified time; eight o' clock came and went without the driver showing any inclination to get going. Third misconception: that it would be nice and warm - the brazier was removed and the temperature plummeted like a stone.

"Only after all the seats were filled did the driver finally think about getting underway. At last, the door was closed. We're off. Or maybe not. After several attempts to start the engine, it was clear that we weren't off. Our driver hauled out a bag of spanners and other miscellaneous implements, got out, opened the bonnet, then fifteen minutes and numerous clunks later, returned. This time the engine started, thank goodness. At last we were actually departing but over streets of compacted snow and ice at a slightly worrying speed. We soon joined a toll road and the bus sped up further, this having the effect of cooling the bus interior to approximately that of the outside temperature, as the bus was unheated. Those thermals that had been prematurely shed were hastily put back on and the idea of drinking any of the water was abandoned – it froze, and anyway the thought of needing to go to the loo but being unable to do so was too off-putting. We certainly wouldn't be sweating it out. The distance between bulkheads was designed for Chinese and insufficient for taller Westerners to lay straight so we lay uncomfortably on the berth, me attempting to get as close as possible to Gordon to benefit from any body warmth but without him thinking I was up to anything else. And so the night passed – sleepless and by far the coldest and most uncomfortable we've yet experienced. At some point during the journey the bus stopped at a filling station and practically everyone bailed out to urinate against a wall, which bore the frozen evidence of previous visits. However, the discomfort of the journey was more than offset by our surprise and relief when we jumped off at an out of town bus station in Beijing the following morning to find it was only a ten-minute taxi ride to the airport. A memorable journey for all the wrong reasons but it did the job."

Platform vendors, Baofeng, January 2003. AF

8th mine, Pingdingshan, October 2003. GE

QJ6792 at Xilin station, March 1997. GE

QJ6792 again; the train is the Nancha to Yichun passenger, March 1997. GE

JS 8122 arrives at the unusually ornate station at Dazhuangkuang with the
morning train from Hanzhuang to Zhongxin. Pingdingshan, January 2003. GE

(right) Going home. The afternoon train from
Hegang departs Fuli, January 2007. AF

QJ 6262 pauses at Nancha station with a refrigerated train for Jiamusi, March 1997. GE

One of the last examples of a steam to steam loco exchange on a China Rail passenger train: QJ 6904 waits
to take over from QJ 6154 on a westbound train at Jixi, March 1999. JT

C4 no. 96 at Guiyang with the mixed train to Jiahe, Chenzhou, November 2001. AF

Zhongxin station, Shuangyashan. Train 72 from Fushan has arrived behind QJ 6805, whilst QJ 6897 runs past, December 2000. AF

A new station but still manual loading of goods at Jingpeng. QJs 6851 and 6577 leave with an eastbound train, January 2004. JT

Narrow gauge in Beijing and the North-East

The north-east of China used to be home to a considerable number of steam-hauled narrow gauge railways – the majority of these being forestry operations that only really got going during the winter logging season. Many closed during the 1990s as the forests became worked out. In 1998 over 4000 people died in China from flooding as a result of excessive deforestation. The reaction was to introduce a ban on logging, and this has led to almost all of the remaining forestry railways being closed down. However, the growth of the Chinese economy has been accompanied by a substantial growth in the demand for timber, which is now being met by a huge increase in imports from eastern Russia and south-east Asia. So potential problems are building up in other countries, but that's a different story.

By the new millennium only a handful of logging lines remained, along with a few other narrow gauge lines for mineral traffic. A surprising survivor, until its closure in 2005 was the Dahuichang limestone railway, a short line only 40 minutes from the centre of Beijing.

In later years the best known of the forestry railways was at Weihe, almost 200 kilometres east of Harbin. In addition to the log trains, this attractive line ran a passenger service, which even included a coach with soft seating. Typically four trains of empties would leave Weihe in the morning to collect logs. The ground in the forests was frozen during winter and this made it easier to drag the logs to the loading points, a task that was often carried out by oxen or bullocks. Simple mechanical winches or even just a team of labourers at the loading points would then lift the logs onto wagons. Most of the loaded trains were scheduled to return after dark, but timings were always very approximate and with disruption due to snow, derailments or other delays frequent, daylight running was common. Weihe was the last steam-hauled logging line to close and succumbed in 2003.

Like main line and industrial steam, standardisation of narrow gauge locomotive types meant that by the late 1990s almost all narrow gauge lines used just one class of locomotive – the C2. This engine was very similar to designs used in Russia and Poland and construction continued in several workshops until the late 1980s. All the narrow gauge lines were 762mm (2 feet 6 inches) gauge.

The last narrow gauge line in the north-east with steam traction was at Huanan in Heilongjiang province, which was built as a forestry railway but stopped moving timber several years ago. It was a remarkable survivor, and although spending several months each year out of use, it managed to continue after logging ended due to the presence of a number of small coal mines near one of its lines - the railway took the output from these mines to a power station at Huanan. The

Manhandling of logs in the yard at Weihe, March 1999. JT

absence of a viable road between mines and power station probably helped the line's longevity.

Leaving Huanan, the line traversed a flat agricultural landscape for some distance before reaching the town of Tuoyaozi. It then climbed into the hills, snaked its way through woods to the summit and descended to Lixin. From Lixin to the end of the line was a gentle descent. A road paralleled the line most of the way to Tuoyaozi; after that you were on foot. There used to be a daily passenger service with railcar, but the service changed and was no longer daily. Then the management decided to increase the fare by a factor of ten for foreigners. Typically there were three trains each way, fairly evenly spread over a 24-hour period. In winter this meant that most of the activity was after dark.

Adrian and John were fortunate enough to stay at private accommodation in Tuoyaozi, albeit on separate occasions. The house had four rooms and two of these had kangs. A kang was a large platform, often taking up half the room, with a concrete top; it was hollow underneath. A stove was kept alight underneath, which kept it warm; it was used as a seat during the day and a bed at night. The family all used the larger kang during our stay and the smaller one was made available for the foreigners. Adrian remarked "I'm not sure whether they were normally as hot as that or whether the family didn't want the foreign guests to get cold, but this thing was absolutely roasting. Lying on a concrete block with the minimum of bedding was also extremely hard and uncomfortable so I soon had the entire contents of my rucksack out to provide some additional padding and insulation from the heat. In December it was dark by four, the family made us a meal at five, they then watched television for a little and went to bed. We had a few beers, wrote some notes and then did the same, but having to lie on this thing for twelve hours or so was torture. Although Tuoyaozi was quite a large village, there was no night life of any description, no street lighting and by 8 p.m. all the lights were out in the village. I have never seen the stars in the night sky so clearly as during that visit. Despite the discomfort of the kang, staying there was a wonderful experience".

There probably wasn't a single house in Tuoyaozi with an indoor toilet and many were communal facilities. Toilets, especially in rural areas, were not China's strong point. Ours was quite standard - a small rickety wooden enclosure, this one without a roof, and with the walls stopping a quarter of a metre short of the ground. There was no plumbing and no water; in fact there was no toilet. Two pieces of timber were provided on which to position the feet and the area behind dug out to accommodate the build-up. A squatting position was adopted. At least everything was frozen in winter so the smell wasn't so offensive but the timber was slippery and there was no lighting after nightfall. Plenty of potential for a mishap, although the illumination from the clear nights and bright stars did at least mean that the hazards were visible. That just left the joy of exposing oneself at -30°C!

C2 no. 21043 stands in front of Huanan shed, January 2001. GE

Loading logs at Lixin, Huanan, December 2001. AF

C2 no. 16 on empties, Xilin mineral railway, March 1997. AF

116

Weihe-bound logs pass Dongfeng, January 2001. GE

Awaiting departure from the limestone loading point, Dahuichang limestone railway, Beijing, December 2004. AF

Activity in the loco yard at the Zhanhe logging railway, March 1999. JT

Empties head away from Weihe, January 2002. AF   Clearing ash from the yard at Huanan, C2 no. 055 behind, March 1999. JT

Coal empties make their way along the main thoroughfare through Tuoyaozi village, Huanan, December 2003. AF

C2 nos. 10 and 309 with a heavily loaded train on the Yabuli logging system, March 1999. JT

C2 no. 55 shunts logs into a mill siding between Zhenzhu and Weihe, January 2001. GE

Steelworks

A third of the world's steel is now produced in China and the demand for it has seen world prices rocket. The largest steelworks in China is at Anshan, south of Shenyang. In 2005 it combined with a steelworks at nearby Benxi to form a group with an annual iron and steel output of over 20 million tonnes. By comparison, the whole British steel output for that year was just over 13 million tonnes and the whole of Europe, 233 million. In 2007, China was expected to produce approximately 470 million tonnes of crude steel.

The pollution from the steelworks could be dreadful and the plant at Anshan was in the middle of a big city. Both Anshan and Benxi steelworks made use of SY class locomotives in the blast furnace areas for moving cauldron wagons containing molten steel or slag. At Anshan two more unusual types, the smaller PL and YJ classes were used where clearances were restricted. Although many steelworks tipped the slag into water, a process that meant it could be used in the manufacture of cement, at Anshan some of the surplus was taken to a slag tipping area. The cauldron part of the wagon was able to rotate, allowing the bright orange molten slag to pour out and down an embankment, a spectacular and antiquated operation. A crane with ball weight was on hand if necessary to thump the base of the cauldron and encourage any remaining solidified residue out.

Adrian visited Anshan steelworks with a group led by Derek Phillips in November 1997. They had overnighted in Shenyang and were driven down the highway to Anshan the next morning. Relatively mild up to that point, the temperature had dropped during the night and it was cold and windy that morning. The city of Anshan was promoting its '1997 - Year of Tourism' campaign and it had been determined that amongst the group was the 10 000th foreign visitor to the city that year, something evidently considered rather special. Their coach was about an hour late by the time it got to the Anshan slip road, and they were met there by a reception party of officials and about 20 girls in smart uniforms, looking frozen to the bone, holding an 'Anshan welcomes its 10 000th foreign visitor' banner. After the necessary handshaking and formalities, the group continued to the steelworks, where SY class locomotives were at work shunting molten steel and molten slag around the blast furnace area. The levels of pollution were quite staggering with just about every colour of smoke belching from one of the many chimneys at some time during the day. By the time they departed, the group was mostly cold, filthy from all the grime and pollution, generally dishevelled, tired and in need of some hot food. But they didn't get away that easily. Because this group was special, they were then given the cultural tour, including a visit to the Anshan jade Buddha - apparently the largest in the world - and an art gallery of traditional Chinese paintings. Only then were they taken to a restaurant – without having had the opportunity to clean up - where the reception party of

SY at Anshan steelworks, November 1999. GE

Benxi steelworks pollution, December 2004. JT

immaculately-dressed civic dignitaries including the mayor, and a television film crew to record the event, surely must have wondered who on earth this collection of tramps was that had arrived.

129

Loading slag wagons at Anshan steelworks, February 1998. JT

(left) Chengde steelworks branch. The prison behind the train made this a contentious location for photography with frequent arrests! February 1998. JT

Chengde again. Three locos work a heavy train of iron ore through the outskirts of town, February 1998. JT

An SY awaits its next duty at Benxi steelworks, December 2004. AF

SY 0833 shunts cauldrons at Anshan, November 1997. AF

The final climb to the summit on the Chengde steelworks branch. The lineside was black with coal dust that showered out of the exhaust of the struggling locos, and a regular flow of locals turned up to gather the bounty, February 1998. JT

YJ 2-6-2 289 in light steam as spare loco at Anshan steelworks, February 1998. JT

SY 0900 shunts at Anshan steelworks, November 1999. GE

Thoroughfare through the middle of Handan steelworks and SY 1535, September 2003. AF

The JiTong railway – the last great steam show on earth?

Were Kodak or Fuji ever aware of this railway, or its significance? Probably not, but they sold tens of thousands of films because of it.

For ten years the Jining Nan to Tongliao (JiTong) railway line was considered by many international steam enthusiasts to have been the saviour of main line steam. Its discovery by Julien Blanc in 1996 coincided with the tail end of main line steam in China. As steam activity declined across the rest of China and the rest of the world, railway enthusiasts from around the globe flocked in ever increasing numbers to this remarkable line to witness and photograph what had become a unique operation.

China's longest local railway, some 943 kilometres in length, was built across Inner Mongolia and opened in December 1995 to regular traffic. Mostly running through sparsely populated landscape, it was primarily constructed for through freight traffic between the north and north-east so that it would avoid the busy routes to and around Beijing. The railway was single track throughout with passing loops at each station and with the exception of a few larger towns, all the stations were equipped with mechanical rather than colour-light signals. It was entirely steam worked using approximately 100 QJ class locomotives purchased second hand from China Rail - this helped reduce the line's capital and running costs. The cost of new diesel locomotives would have been several times higher than that of overhauled QJs, many of which were less than ten years old at the time. New steam locomotive workshops were constructed at Daban, part way along the line although, in common with practise elsewhere, most normal servicing was carried out in the open. The line was split into five sections for operation, with locomotive changes at the start and end of each. Although most of the landscape was quite flat, the central section from Daban to Haoluku included the 'Jingpeng Pass', by far the most spectacular part of the railway, with horseshoe curves, tunnels and sweeping viaducts. Because of the gradients involved, the majority of trains over this section were double-headed. Initially, traffic over the line was light but it built up steadily and additional passing places were constructed to increase the line's capacity.

In winter when the steam exhaust was visible, trains could be seen approaching and snaking around the different levels of the pass for more than an hour. It was estimated that during the final winters, as many as 4000 international enthusiasts visited this line to enjoy the spectacle. Many visited several times hoping for those

QJ 6388 by the water column at Jingpeng station, November 1999. JT

ideal but elusive photographic conditions of fresh snow, still air, clear skies, low sunlight and a train at just the right moment. What most got was strong winds, which when combined with extreme cold, made the exercise something of an endurance test to the point where cases of frostbite were not unknown.

Most visitors stayed in the village of Reshui on the eastern side of the Jingpeng Pass, where a growing number of hotels handled the influx. The hotels weren't built exclusively for railway enthusiasts, however. The name Reshui translates as 'hot water'; it is a spa town and is apparently very busy with Chinese visitors during summer. The hot water supply in many hotels came directly from the spas and as a result the central heating systems were overwhelmingly efficient. John insisted on sleeping with the window open despite the outside temperature being in the minus twenties. The water had a characteristic sulphurous smell and slightly slimy feel. On one visit, Gordon and Adrian shared a room in Reshui. After spending a day out in the chill winds, the perfect recuperation was a hot bath (followed by a few beers, of course) and the bathroom was thoughtfully equipped with two baths so neither had to wait for the other. Ah, what joy, the stink of sulphur in the air, and the hot water relaxing the muscles and driving away the aches and pains; now where were those beers?

Sadly, traffic levels continued to rise to the point where new diesels, with their ability to haul heavier trains, became not only viable but necessary. By December 2005, exactly ten years after the opening of the line, the show was over - the last revenue-earning main line steam runs were made and dieselisation was complete.

Jining Nan to Tongliao passenger train destination board. AF

Traditional freight movement near Lindong, November 2004. GE

Crossing barrier mechanism near Lindong, January 2005. AF

The signalman at the east end of Xiakengzi station watches attentively as QJ's 6828 and 7112 approach on an eastbound freight, January 2004. JT

A woman in Erdi village calls in her pigs for their evening feed as two unidentified
QJs make the eastbound climb towards the summit at Shangdian, January 2004. JT

(right) QJs 6639 & 6630 head east near Xiakengzi, November 1999. GE

QJs 6853 & 6996 on westbound freight climbing towards the summit between Diaojiaduan and Yamenmiao, January 2005. AF

QJs 6851 and 6577 shortly after leaving Jingpeng station gather as much speed as possible for the long climb ahead, January 2004. JT

QJs 6773 and 6630 approach the new station at Hatashan with an eastbound train, January 2004. JT

Unidentified QJs head west across Jingpeng viaduct just after sunrise, January 2004. JT

QJ's 7009 & 6389 approach Shangdian summit, November 1999. GE

Unidentified QJ's on the final stretch towards Shangdian summit with an eastbound train, January 2004. JT

Daban shed, arguably the world's last main line steam depot, closed to steam in December 2005. January 2005. JT

QJ's 6389 and 7009 on the eastbound ascent of the Jingpeng pass near tunnel, 4. November 1999. JT

A single QJ with a westbound departure from Lindong, January 2004. JT

At little more than a plod, QJ 7112 heads west out of Lindong with a heavy load, January 2005. AF

Industrial survivors

At the time of writing, steam still survives at a handful of industrial locations scattered across north and north-east China. Unsurprisingly these are mostly coal mining operations and two of these are large opencast mines, where there is the likelihood that steam will last the longest.

Between Beijing and Shenyang are two industrial steam railways that lay unknown (to Westerners) until the beginning of this century – the Huludao Limestone Railway and Nanpiao Mining Railway. From Jinzhou, on the main line between Beijing and Shenyang, a branch heads north to the town of Nanpiao, where China Rail ends and the mining railway begins. This railway was a remarkable discovery by Louis Cerny in August 2003. The mines' railway has two branches, each of which has some steep gradients to take it through the hilly terrain, consequently the trains are quite short. Both branches have a passenger service, which could either be steam or diesel, the railway having some SY class and three old ex China Rail diesels. This is a fascinating area with large and somewhat decrepit old mines nestled in the hills served by the railway, along with numerous small mines with their little tubs.

Another relatively recent mines railway 'discovery', but with a completely different character is the Meihekou Mine Railway, north-east of Shenyang. Again, there is a connection to China Rail and two branches, and like Nanpiao there is also a passenger service but this little system traverses flat landscape, and often runs unfenced alongside a road. In contrast to the gritty feel of Nanpiao with its grimy locomotives, this area is somewhat smarter and the locomotives, two of which are decorated, are kept clean and appear well looked after. Although lacking any dramatic scenery, this railway has a certain charm of its own. Adrian remarked that kangs excepted, the hotel in Yijing - the main town and headquarters of the mines railway - had the hardest beds he had ever encountered in China.

At Fuxin, between Nanpiao and Shenyang, an industrial railway system served an opencast mine and a number of deep mines. The opencast mine has now been worked out and ceased operation. Several years ago, John visited Fuxin and relates the following:

"As I relaxed in the hotel lounge, I was approached by a young man who introduced himself as the Assistant Manager, and he turned out to be the only person who spoke any really useful English. There was obviously some concern. It appeared that I was the first Westerner to turn up at the hotel without a Chinese guide in tow. I explained I was there to photograph the steam locomotives, and he wanted to know how I planned to get about. I said I would like to buy a map and hire a bicycle. In a land of so many bicycles, it did not occur that this would be a problem, but there were none for hire in Fuxin.

He thought a moment and then announced 'The hotel will buy a bicycle and

An ashpicker wheels away his bag of scavenged coal pieces from the stabling point at Xiamiaozi, Nanpiao, December 2004. JT

you can hire it from us'. He also wrote out a note for me, which was basically an SOS. As I understood it, if I had a problem of any sort, I hand the note to someone, and it requested them to phone the hotel on my behalf so that he could sort out the difficulty. He could not have been more helpful, though with what they charged me for the hire, I suspect I had purchased the bike for them by the time I left.

With an assurance that it was 'quality China bicycle', I set forth at dawn next morning, joining the throngs of locals pedalling their way to work. I attracted surprisingly little attention, apart from a few quick double takes.

The saddle was the first thing to work loose. Each of the four days I used the bicycle, at least one thing worked dangerously loose, or fell off completely. Admittedly, the item that fell off on the fourth day was me, so the subsequent problem with the pedal was not the fault of the bike that time.

I never had to resort to my SOS note. I soon discovered that every few hundred yards there was to be found a bicycle repair man. Some were more easy to spot than others; some were just an old man sat by the side of the road, identifiable only by a couple of inner tubes or a wheel laying alongside them. But they all had their stock of 'bits', usually in a big old biscuit tin. So you wheeled your faulty charge to them, pointed to the problem and left them to sort it out. They invariably needed a replacement nut or bolt, so a large sheet of newspaper was laid on the pavement, the biscuit tin was emptied on to it, and out of this heap of nuts, bolts, odds and ends would emerge the required spare. One man laboured for the best part of half an hour to get me back on the road again (it was a puncture this time), and then charged me 1 yuan. I had nothing smaller than a 10 and he had no change. Even at 10 Yuan it was less than £1, and I was very grateful to him, but he would not take my money and insisted I wait while he rustled up the change from his neighbours."

The greatest concentrations of working steam locomotives left in China are to be found at two substantial opencast mines, both in remote parts of the country - one to the north and one to the west.

Manzhouli in Inner Mongolia is a lively trading town on the Russian border. At the border railway station, Chinese standard gauge lines meet the Russian broad gauge. Cross border freight is important and there are extensive facilities here for changing wagon bogies to permit them to make the onward journey. It is believed that a number of broad gauge QJ class locomotives were specially constructed to carry out these shunting duties, but they have long since been displaced by diesels. Not far from Manzhouli, lies Jalainur and its huge opencast mine. The scale of this mining operation has to be seen to be believed. A series of terraces allow the tracks to zig-zag their way down one side of the 'hole' to gain access to the thick coal seams. Standing at one end, it is possible to see the exhausts of ten or so SY class locomotives working in the 'hole'. Spoil trains are constantly moving up the zig-zags, alternately pushing then pulling their train to get out of the top and to the spoil tip, whilst trains of empties are doing the reverse. When pushing the train, the driver has limited visibility so a lookout with red and green flags stands in the end vehicle of each train to warn of danger. These lookouts have a tough job - they must stand motionless in the end wagon with no protection from the weather, in temperatures which in winter regularly drop well below -30°C. The coal trains don't usually come out of the hole; instead they make their way to a shed building at one end, where the coal is discharged onto an underground conveyor which takes it to a washery. Mining is carried out around the clock and an active fleet of approximately 30 SY class locomotives work the 'hole' and a handful of nearby deep mines.

A coal yard in Jalainur is supplied by the mining railway and from there, distribution around the town is carried out by horse and cart. Wagons with side doors are pushed into the yard by SY locomotives and are manually emptied by gangs with shovels. The horse-drawn carts are loaded, often by teams of women, sometimes with the help of the male driver. The women are easily distinguishable as they always wear scarves across their faces to help protect them from inhaling the dust, the men take no such precautions. A steady stream of horses and carts come and go although this is no longer exclusively their preserve; a number of small lorries are also loaded there.

Way out west near Hami in Xinjiang province is Sandaoling opencast mine. It is similar to Jalainur but instead of SY, it uses JS class locomotives. Both systems have locomotive workshops which are capable of carrying out heavy overhauls – this puts them in a stronger position to keep steam than many of the other industrial survivors, and they are likely to be amongst the very last users of revenue-earning steam in the world.

The layer of frost on horses delivering coal at Jalainur suggests they may have been kept outside overnight when temperatures dropped well below - 30°C, December 2005. JT

Sunset at the tipping area. Sandaoling opencast mine near Hami, November 2005. GE

SY 1217 is ready to depart Yijing with coal for the China Rail exchange yard at Heishantou. Meihekou mining railway, January 2005. AF

JS6243 waits for banking assistance before departing with limestone empties and coal. Huludao limestone railway, December 2004. AF

The coal yard at Jalainur. Both men and women labour to unload coal by hand from the railway wagons and transfer it to horse carts for delivery around the town, December 2005. JT

Early morning, December 2005. JT

SY1448 brings in more coal, December 2005. JT

A woman assists with the loading, December 2005. JT

The weighbridge, December 2005. JT

163

Mining activity continues through the night at Jalainur opencast pit, December 2005. JT

SY 1047 passes a copper smelting plant at Baiyin, November 2005. GE

An SY runs light engine from Fuxin power station, February 1998. JT

Two crossing keepers stand to attention as JS8352 departs Gusheng with the single-coach morning passenger service. Hekounan, November 2005. GE

SY 1092 on the 09:45 short passenger working from Hungjia to Xiamiaozi passing Hungjia market, Nanpiao, January 2007. AF

Jalainur washery, March 1997. AF

SY 1478 pulls away from Weizigou washery bound for Sanjiazi. Nanpiao, January 2004. AF

The tipping area at Sandaoling opencast mine, November 2005. GE

(next page) SY1217 departs Yijing, Meihekou mining railway, January 2005. AF

171

SY 0150 crosses the Datong river on a train for the alumina works, Yaojie, November 2005. GE

Photographers´ Note

Medium-format camera gear was used for the main photographs in this book.

In the early days, John used a Bronica SQA 6x6 but this soon became the spare camera to a SQAi with power-wind. Lenses were different combinations from 50mm, 80mm, 150mm, 180mm and 250mm, but never on the same trip or he wouldn't have been able to lift the bag off the ground. A remote battery pack was deployed whenever it was likely to be cold. That for the SQA was totally inadequate, the thin flimsy cables snapping at low temperature but the one for the SQAi (actually manufactured for the defunct SQAM), with its six batteries and heavy cables was much better.

Gordon and Adrian used Mamiya 645s.

Gordon had the Mamiya 'Super' and 'Pro' bodies with 45mm, 80mm, 150mm, and occasionally 210mm lenses and a 2-times converter. After experiencing so many problems with both these cameras, he purchased an older 1000s camera body for his later visits, although he freely admits that dropping them so many times (usually when slipping on ice), probably didn't help matters.

From 1999, Adrian used Mamiya 1000s bodies with variously 45mm, 50mm shift, 80mm, 110mm, 150mm and 210mm lenses. Although older than the 'Super' and 'Pro' models, he considered the 1000s to be more durable. Often two cameras would be mounted on a bracket so that the scene could be captured on slide and black & white film simultaneously. Prior to this he had a Bronica ETRS and 50mm, 75mm and 150mm lenses, but he soon went off the Bronica's leaf shutters, and those pesky dark slides.

Adrian made some remote battery packs in case low temperatures caused the camera battery output to become too feeble, but they were only ever used once. Generally, we were pleasantly surprised at how well the camera batteries did perform in the difficult conditions. Lots of spares were always carried, however.

Most of the time the cameras were steadied with a tripod or a monopod. In conditions of extreme cold holding a monopod or tripod would lead to the heat being drawn out of the hand even when wearing thick ski-type gloves, so padding was wrapped around and secured to part of the monopod or tripod leg to prevent this. All the tight fitting plastic covers and caps on Adrian's tripod became loose and fell off in the extreme cold (evidently plastic contracts more than aluminium in the cold). Fortunately these parts were only cosmetic.

We all used colour slide film, predominantly Fuji ISO 100 Provia, initially RDPII and then the newer RDP III. In more recent years, this film was usually uprated to ISO 200. Fuji Velvia 50 (rated at 80) and Provia 400 were also used but less frequently. John exclusively took colour slides, but Adrian also used black & white negative film – mostly Ilford HP5, and on the earlier trips also the 'chromogenic' Ilford XP2 and occasionally Kodak's equivalent, BW400CN. Gordon also initially used HP5 and then the now-discontinued Afga Scala black & white slide film.

Much of this equipment suffered on various occasions from the combination of abuse and low temperatures that it was subjected to during our visits. When Adrian contacted Mamiya for advice and precautions for using their equipment at low temperatures, their recommendation was not to use it below freezing point – advice which was promptly ignored.

Being outside meant that the temperature of the camera gear soon dropped to that of the surroundings. It was therefore essential to pack the gear back in the camera bag before going into the warmth. Popping into a noodle bar for lunch would otherwise result in the camera getting covered in condensation, which would then turn to ice. The equipment would then be useless until the ice had thawed and condensation evaporated or wiped off.

Changing lenses or film was very difficult in extreme cold but had to be done outside to prevent the formation of condensation or ice inside the camera. Even with medium format gear, these tasks could only be done without gloves, and the colder the fingers got, the clumsier they became and the longer it took to do. There have been several reports of 35mm users getting scratches on their film, possibly as a result of ice crystals in the film compartment. Fortunately the medium-format 120 roll film never suffered from this, perhaps because of its backing paper.

A variety of problems occurred with the equipment. When the shutter didn't fire, or part of a mechanism jammed, this was very frustrating but at least it was clear that something was wrong and attempts could be made to sort it out. Much worse were more subtle faults, where the equipment didn't exhibit any outward signs of being faulty and so no corrective action was implemented. These faults were only discovered back home after the films had been processed. The main offender in this latter category was the 'lazy iris', in which the lens failed to shutdown to the correct stop, resulting in severely overexposed images with minimal depth of field. This problem has occurred on the Mamiya 80mm and 150mm lenses and also on the Bronica 150mm lens. It was an easy problem to overcome if aware of it – on the Mamiya lenses, they could be switched to manual setting, and on the Bronica, the depth-of-field preview lever depressed when the shutter was fired.

The slides or negatives have all been digitised. Most of the images from colour slides remain colour, but a few have been converted to black & white and then toned. The black & white images have been toned to varying degrees.

Acknowledgements

We were not really explorers. We didn't find any new steam sites during our visits. Limited time and the desire to maximise photographic opportunities whilst out there meant that we went to places that we had information about and we are therefore indebted to other people for this information. It primarily came from internet sites such as Rob Dickinson's 'International working steam' and Florian Menius' 'QJ Country' (now Dave Fielding's SY-Country) and the associated 'Steam in China' newsgroup, which in turn relied on visitors sending reports of their trips, and also the reports and maps from Bernd Seiler's 'Farrail' and Duncan Cotterill's 'Railography' sites. The journals 'World Steam' and 'Continental Railway Journal' also provided much useful information.

SY 0754 puts up an all-out effort to make it over the hill beyond Zaojiatun without stalling. Nanpiao, December 2004. AF

Special thanks are due to the following people:

Bryan Acford, Julien Blanc, Louis Cerny, Duncan Cotterill, Rob Dickinson, Bruce Evans, Florian Menius, Derek Phillips, Bernd Seiler, and everyone else who has been to China and went to the trouble of reporting what they saw for the benefit of others. John Summerill for his patient scanning of many of our medium format transparencies. Alan Stevens for proof reading our waffle.

Don White for his good company, and everyone else who has shared our travels at one time or another. The Chinese guides that we have turned to, notably the indomitable Mrs Sun, and Zebedee, the best guide in Sichuan province.

Inspiration

The work of Colin Gifford
'All trains to stop' by Hans Steeneken
Nothing to do with railways, but 'Ghosts in the Wilderness – Abandoned America' by Tony & Eva Worobiec

Warning sign, Jixi. AF

CHINA - North, East
● Featured locations

Zhanhe
Bei'an
Jalainur

Yichun
Xilin
Nancha
Jiamusi
Huanan
Harbin
Weihe

Hegang
Shuang-
yashan
Jixi
Yabuli

Da'an

Chaoyangchuan
Changchun
Hunjiang   Songshuzhen
Meihekou
Tonghua

Lindong
Daban
Jingpeng

Shenyang
Fuxin   Benxi

Yebaishou
Nanpiao
Chengde   Anshan

Huludao

Baotou   Shiguai   Beijing

Tianjin